THE WORLD'S TOP TEN

RIVERS

Neil Morris

ILLUSTRATED BY VANESSA CARD

RSVP

**RAINTREE
STECK-VAUGHN**
P U B L I S H E R S
The Steck-Vaughn Company

Austin, Texas

Words in **bold** are explained in the glossary
on pages 30–31.

Text copyright © Neil Morris 1997
Illustrations copyright © Vanessa Card 1997
© Copyright 1997 Steck-Vaughn Company

Published by Raintree Steck-Vaughn Publishers, an imprint
of Steck-Vaughn Company

Editors: Claire Edwards, Helene Resky
Designer: Dawn Apperley
Picture researcher: Juliet Duff
Consultant: Elizabeth M. Lewis

Picture acknowledgments: J. Allan Cash: 14. Comstock:
25 top George Gerster. Eye Ubiquitous: 5 bottom, 8, 9, 18,
29 bottom. Robert Harding Picture Library: 10, 12, 13, 19,
28 bottom, 29 top. Hutchison Library: 15. NHPA: 28 top.
Russia and Republics Photo Library: 27 Mark Wadlow.
Still Pictures: 5 top, 11, 16 Bios, 21, 23, 26. Tony Stone
Images: 22. Trip: 17, 20, 25 bottom.

Library of Congress Cataloging-in-Publication Data
Morris, Neil.
    Rivers / Neil Morris; illustrated by Vanessa Card.
      p.   cm. — (The worlds's top ten)
    Includes index.
    Summary: Provides information about the
surroundings, course, and importance of ten of the
world's longest rivers, including the Nile, the Mississippi,
the Yenisei, and the Paraná.
    ISBN 0-8172-4338-0
    1. Rivers — Juvenile literature.   [1. Rivers.]
I. Card, Vanessa, ill. II. Title. III. Series.
GB1203.8.M67 1997
910'.916'93 — dc20   96-642
                                    CIP AC

Printed in Hong Kong
Bound in the United States
1 2 3 4 5 6 7 8 9 0   99 98 97 96

Contents

What Is a River?

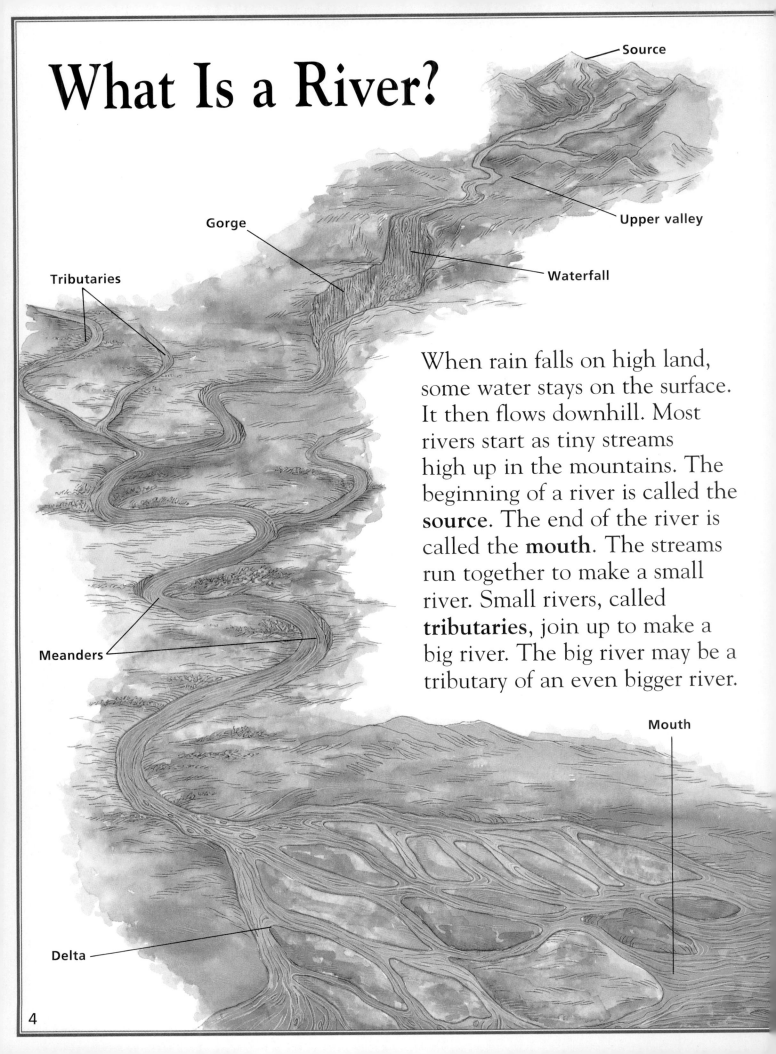

Source

Upper valley

Gorge

Waterfall

Tributaries

Meanders

Mouth

Delta

When rain falls on high land, some water stays on the surface. It then flows downhill. Most rivers start as tiny streams high up in the mountains. The beginning of a river is called the **source**. The end of the river is called the **mouth**. The streams run together to make a small river. Small rivers, called **tributaries**, join up to make a big river. The big river may be a tributary of an even bigger river.

Flowing to the ocean

As water flows, it wears away the land and makes a valley. A river carries the soil and stones it has worn away. The moving soil and stones scrape against the bottom and sides of the riverbed, making it deeper and wider. This is how valleys are made by rivers, but it takes many thousands of years.

Near its source, a river is narrow, shallow, and fast. By the time it reaches the ocean, it seems to move more slowly. But, underneath, the flow of water is strong and dangerous.

A tributary of the Po River tumbles down a mountainside in Italy. As it flows toward the Adriatic Sea, it becomes wider and is dammed to make electricity.

Using rivers

People have always used the water from rivers to help them grow crops. They have also used rivers to travel by boat. Rivers were often the quickest way, or sometimes the only way, to cross large areas of unexplored land. Today we build dams across rivers and use the power of flowing water to make **hydroelectricity**.

Rivers are so important that towns and cities throughout the world have grown up beside them. Today the **waste** from cities often **pollutes** the water.

Towns and villages lie along the banks of the Rhine River, in Germany. Barges carry goods on the river.

The longest rivers

In this book we take a look at the ten longest rivers in the world. We see how they have changed the land and affected the lives of the people who live near them.

5

The Longest Rivers

This map shows the ten longest rivers in the world. Long rivers have many tributaries. Each tributary has a different source and may have a different name from its main river. The main river and all its tributaries are called a **river system**. To find the length of a river, we measure from the source that is farthest from its mouth.

The World's Top Ten Rivers

1	The Nile	4,145 miles
2	The Amazon	4,007 miles
3	The Chang (Yangtze)	3,915 miles
4	The Mississippi-Missouri	3,741 miles
5	The Yenisei	3,442 miles
6	The Huang (Yellow)	3,395 miles
7	The Ob	3,361 miles
8	The Paraná	3,032 miles
9	The Zaire (Congo)	2,920 miles
10	The Lena	2,734 miles

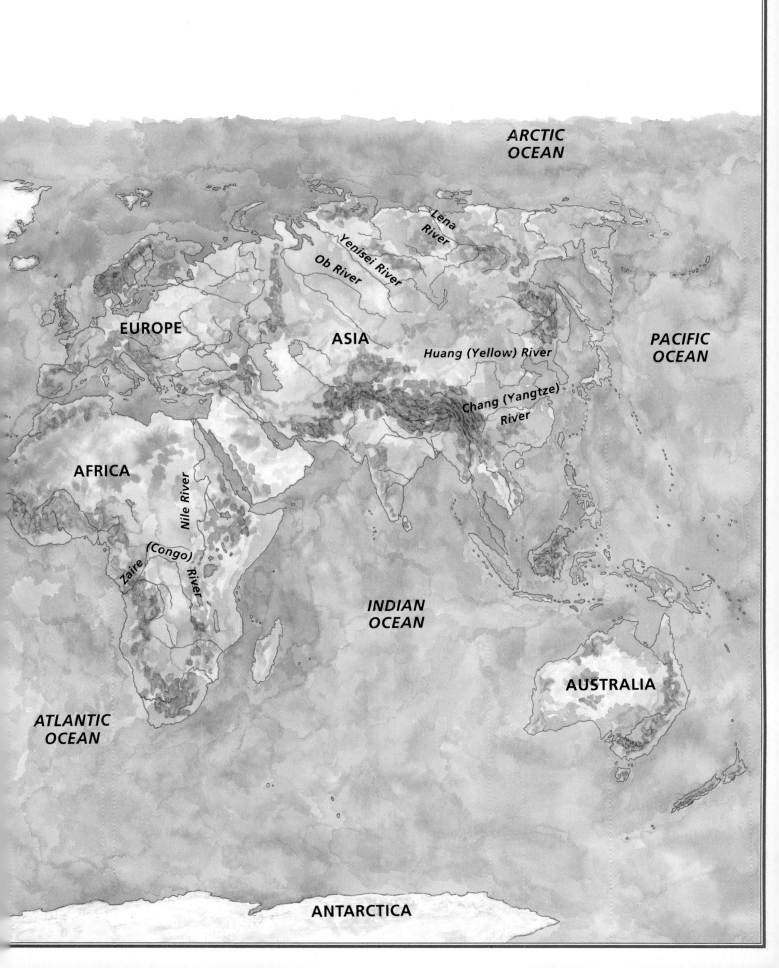

ARCTIC
OCEAN

Lena
River

Yenisei River

Ob River

EUROPE

ASIA

PACIFIC
OCEAN

Huang (Yellow) River

Chang (Yangtze)
River

AFRICA

Nile River

Zaire (Congo) River

INDIAN
OCEAN

AUSTRALIA

ATLANTIC
OCEAN

ANTARCTICA

The Nile

The Nile is the longest river in the world. Its water brings life to the desert countries that it flows through. Most of the people of Egypt live along its banks.

These Egyptian boats with triangular sails use the wind to sail up the Nile and travel back with the strong flow of water.

Journey north

The Nile River has two main branches. They are called the White Nile and the Blue Nile because of the different colors of their waters.

The White Nile begins as the Kagera River in the small African country of Burundi. It runs into Lake Victoria, the largest lake in Africa, and then heads north through swamps and deserts. At Khartoum, the capital of Sudan, the river is joined by the fast-flowing Blue Nile.

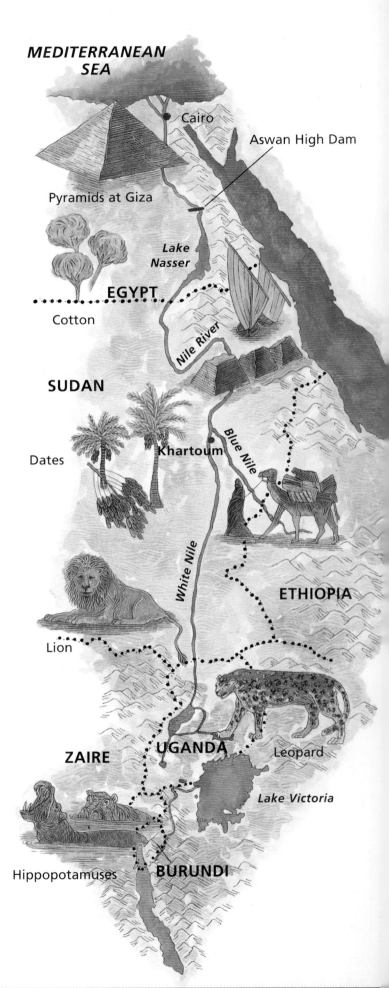

MEDITERRANEAN SEA

Cairo

Aswan High Dam

Pyramids at Giza

Lake Nasser

EGYPT

Cotton

Nile River

SUDAN

Dates

Khartoum

Blue Nile

White Nile

ETHIOPIA

Lion

ZAIRE

UGANDA

Leopard

Lake Victoria

Hippopotamuses

BURUNDI

FACTS
LENGTH   4,145 miles (6,670 km)
SOURCE   Burundi, central Africa
MOUTH   Egypt, into the
          Mediterranean Sea

Land of the pharaohs

The Nile flows through Egypt. Egypt's capital, Cairo, is built on the banks of the Nile, which flows toward the Mediterranean Sea. The ancient Egyptians, whose kingdoms were ruled by **pharaohs**, worshiped the Nile River.

They fished in it, bathed in it, drank its waters, and built tombs and temples on its shores. In ancient times, the river flooded every year. The floods spread fertile mud over the land, helping farmers to grow good crops.

A narrow canal has been dug next to the wide Nile to help water the land. Corn, wheat, rice, and vegetables are important crops in Egypt, and cotton is grown to sell abroad.

Watering the desert

In modern times, people wanted to control the floods, and so dams were built across the Nile River. The biggest dam, the Aswan High Dam, forms Lake Nasser. The lake is more than 300 miles (500 km) long, which is about the distance between St. Louis and Chicago.

The lake stores floodwater for use throughout the year, and the dam provides hydroelectricity. But it also stops fertile mud from moving downstream. This means that modern Egyptians have to use more chemicals to **fertilize** their land.

The Amazon

The Amazon River is not as long as the Nile, but it carries much more water. More than one-fifth of all the water in the world's rivers flows down the Amazon.

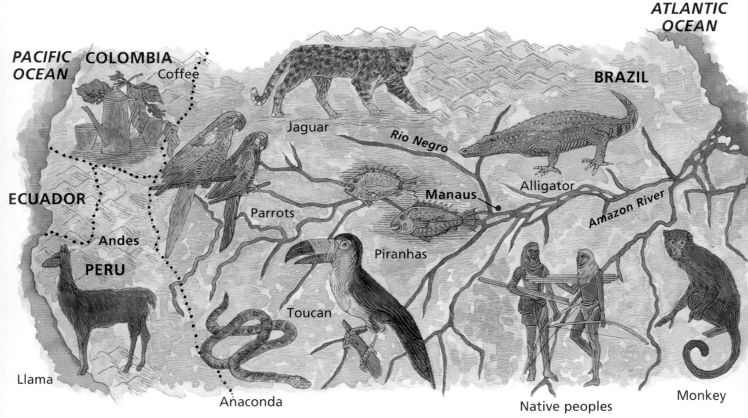

PACIFIC OCEAN

COLOMBIA

Coffee

ATLANTIC OCEAN

BRAZIL

Jaguar

Rio Negro

Alligator

Manaus

Amazon River

Parrots

ECUADOR

Andes

PERU

Piranhas

Toucan

Llama

Anaconda

Native peoples

Monkey

Giant river system

The Amazon is fed by thousands of smaller rivers. By the time it reaches the ocean, it is very wide. The Amazon **delta** is more than 185 miles (300 km) across. In a single second it pours 7,000,000 cubic feet (200,000 m³) of water into the Atlantic Ocean. That is the same amount of water that can be held by a hundred Olympic-size swimming pools.

FACTS
LENGTH   4,007 miles (6,448 km)
SOURCE   Lake Villafro, Peru
MOUTH   Brazil, into the Atlantic Ocean

The Rio Negro joins the Amazon near the city of Manaus. Manaus is an important center of trade and one of Brazil's largest cities. A million people live there.

Melting snow in the Andes and tropical rain cause floods up to 29 feet (9 m) deep in the Amazon rain forest. The floods leave a waterline high up on the trees.

Through the rain forest

The Amazon begins high in the Andes mountains of Peru. It flows across the **plains** of Brazil, through the biggest tropical **rain forest** in the world. Parrots and toucans feed in the treetops by the river, while monkeys swing through the branches.

There are more than 2,000 kinds of fish in the Amazon, from the bright angelfish to the deadly piranha with its razor-sharp teeth. Jaguars hunt by the river, while alligators and snakes swim in search of **prey.**

Many rivers flood when there is very heavy rain or when snow melts near the river's source. Every year the Amazon River floods the huge rain forest.

Amazonian people

Hundreds of years ago, many native groups lived in villages along the Amazon. They ate food from the forest and fished in the river. But whole groups were wiped out when huge areas of forest were cut down for wood or were burned to make way for crops and cattle ranches. Many people are now trying to save the Amazon rain forest.

The Chang

The Chang River is sometimes called the Yangtze. The Chang is the longest river in China and the third longest river in the world.

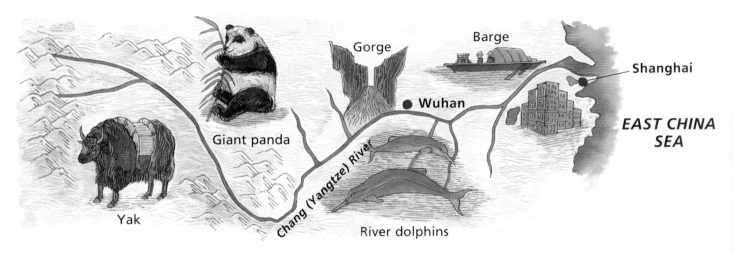

Gorge

Barge

Shanghai

Wuhan

EAST CHINA SEA

Giant panda

Chang (Yangtze) River

Yak

River dolphins

Across China

The Chang begins high in the snow-covered mountains of western China. When the snow melts in the summer, water flows down to the **foothills** and forms streams. The streams then run together to make a river.

More than 700 small rivers join the Chang on its journey across China. At first, the river passes through narrow **gorges**. Then, it becomes wider as it moves over flat land. Finally, the river flows into the East China Sea near Shanghai, China's largest city.

The Xiling Gorge is 47 miles (76 km) long. The river zigzags through the gorge toward one of China's biggest dams, the Gezhouba.

A ferry carries people between Shanghai and the city of Chongqing. There are always many ships on the Chang near the port of Shanghai. They come from all over the world.

FACTS

LENGTH   3,915 miles (6,300 km)
SOURCE   Kunlun Shan, western China
MOUTH   Eastern China, into the East China Sea

Using the river

The Chinese have built dams where the Chang rushes through gorges to turn the power of the water into hydroelectricity. Between the city of Wuhan and the East China Sea, the river is wide and deep enough for big ocean liners. But ferries, **barges**, and **rafts** make up most of the river traffic.

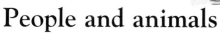

People and animals

Nearly half of China's people live near the banks of the Chang. The river has plenty of fish and is home to dolphins and alligators. **Reserves** have been set up to protect the whitefin river dolphin, but there are probably only a few hundred alligators left in the lower part of the river.

The Mississippi-Missouri

The Mississippi River is the fourth longest river system in the world. The Missouri River is its main tributary.

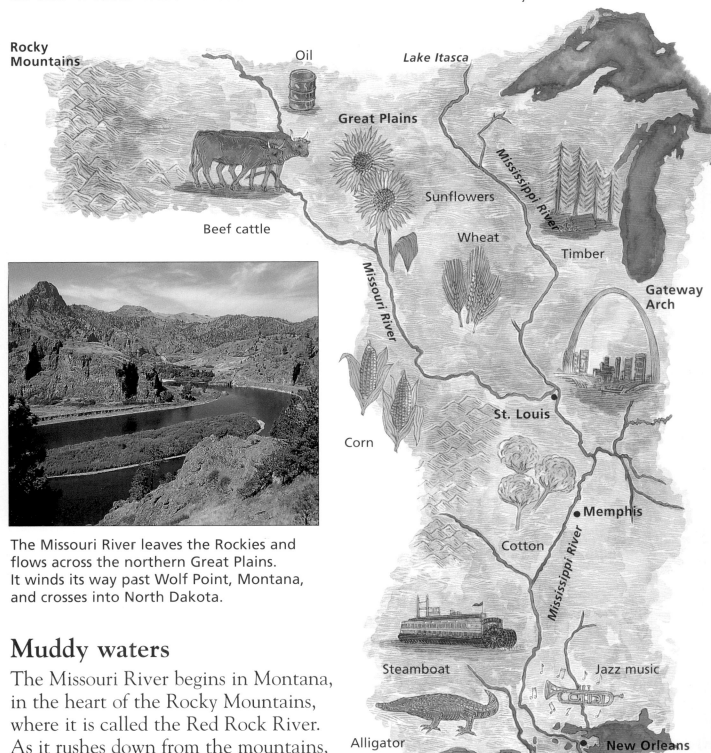

The Missouri River leaves the Rockies and flows across the northern Great Plains. It winds its way past Wolf Point, Montana, and crosses into North Dakota.

Muddy waters

The Missouri River begins in Montana, in the heart of the Rocky Mountains, where it is called the Red Rock River. As it rushes down from the mountains, it picks up a lot of sand and mud. Because of this, the Missouri River has been given the nickname "Big Muddy."

Steamboat river

The source of the Mississippi River is near Lake Itasca, Minnesota. In the language of the local Native Americans, Mississippi means "great river." It flows through the central lowlands of the United States, heading south toward the Gulf of Mexico.

Steamboats started taking goods and passengers up and down the river in 1812. Today the river is still an important route for carrying cargo. Tourists can also travel on the world's largest riverboat, the *Mississippi Queen*, which is 380 feet (116 m) long.

Danger from floods

The Missouri River pours into the Mississippi just north of the city of St. Louis. The river then winds on past Memphis, heading for New Orleans. At this point, the river still has about 112 miles (180 km) to go before it reaches the ocean.

In many places people have built high **embankments** to stop the river from flooding. But in 1993 the worst flood in American history left more than 70,000 families homeless. Houses that were normally 4 miles (6 km) away from the Mississippi disappeared under 16 feet (5 m) of water.

The Mississippi River flows through New Orleans. This modern city is one of the busiest ports in the world. Ships carry goods, such as grain, paper, cotton, iron, and steel.

FACTS

LENGTH 3,741 miles (6,020 km)
SOURCE Lake Itasca, Minnesota
MOUTH Louisiana into the Gulf of Mexico

The Yenisei

The Yenisei is the longest of three big Siberian rivers. It flows from the south of Russia to its northern coast on the Arctic Ocean.

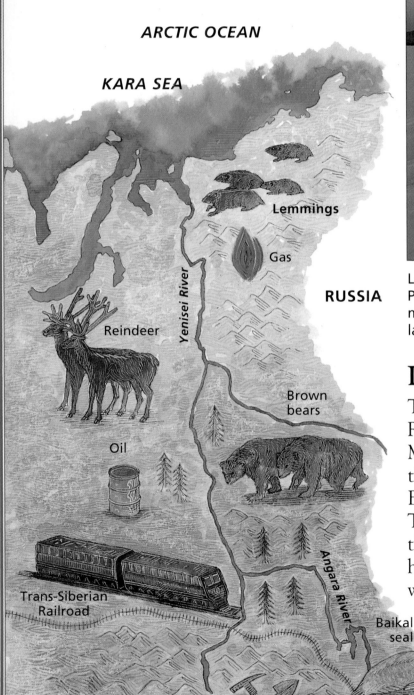

Lake Baikal is frozen by the middle of winter. People fish through holes in the ice, which is more than 5 feet (1.5 m) thick in places. The lake is home to the world's only freshwater seals.

Deepest lake

The Yenisei begins as the Selenga River, near the Russian border with Mongolia. Along with 335 other rivers, the Selenga River flows into Lake Baikal, the deepest lake in the world. This lake holds about one-fifth of all the freshwater on Earth. Lake Baikal has only one outlet, the Angara River, which flows into the Yenisei.

ARCTIC OCEAN

KARA SEA

Lemmings

Gas

RUSSIA

Yenisei River

Reindeer

Oil

Brown bears

Trans-Siberian Railroad

Angara River

Baikal seal

Fish

Lake Baikal

Gold

Selenga River

MONGOLIA

Forest and desert

The Yenisei River runs north through Siberia, a large region of Russia. For most of its journey, it crosses the **taiga**, where reindeer graze. This huge, cold forest is full of **evergreen** trees, such as **fir**, pine, and **larch**. But a few hundred miles from the Arctic Ocean, the land changes. This is the **tundra**, an Arctic desert where the earth is always frozen. Only a few inches on top melt in the summer. It is too cold for trees to grow.

FACTS

LENGTH 3,442 miles (5,540 km)
SOURCE Mongolia–Russia border
MOUTH Russia, into the Kara Sea and the Arctic Ocean

Dams, oil, and minerals

There are many dams that make hydroelectricity on the Yenisei. The hydroelectricity is used to power **steel foundries** and factories. Oil and gas have been found in the region. In 1994 there were large oil spills that polluted Siberian rivers and caused damage to the environment. Gold, silver, and other precious metals are mined here.

The Yenisei River is 186 miles (300 km) south of the Arctic Circle as it flows past this village, which has sprung up between the taiga and the river.

The Huang

The Huang River is the second longest river in China and the sixth longest river in the world. It is also called the "Yellow River." This name comes from its muddy yellow color. The Huang is the world's muddiest river.

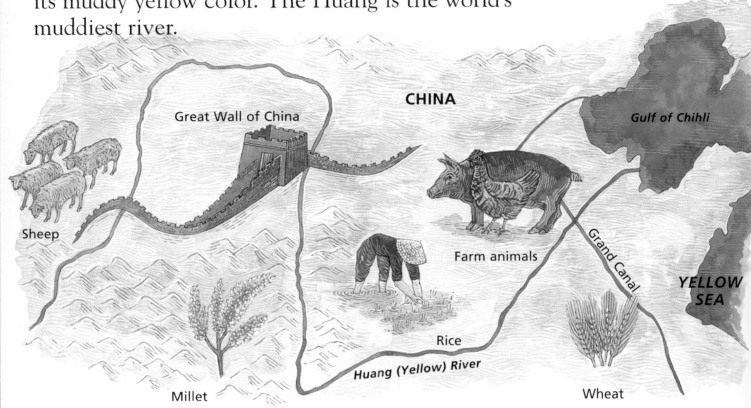

CHINA

Great Wall of China

Sheep

Farm animals

Grand Canal

Gulf of Chihli

YELLOW SEA

Rice

Huang (Yellow) River

Millet

Wheat

Farming along the river

The Huang River begins on a high **plateau** and flows across China to the Gulf of Chihli. The soil around the Huang River is made fertile by the river's muddy **silt**. This makes it ideal farming land. Chinese civilization began here about 9,000 years ago.

Today the main crops are grains, such as wheat, **millet**, and rice. China is the world's greatest producer of wheat and rice. More than two-thirds of Chinese people work on the land.

Land on one side of the Huang River has been used to grow crops.

18

Boats travel on the Huang River. It is easy to see why the muddiest river in the world is called the Yellow River.

People in danger

More than 100 million people live along the Huang River and its tributaries. In some places the river is higher than the surrounding countryside. People have built **dykes** to hold back the water, but the plains are easily flooded. Over the centuries, millions of people have been killed when the river floods. This is why the river is often called "China's sorrow."

Changing course

The Huang River has changed course many times during its history. At different times, it has poured into the Yellow Sea at points as far apart as 500 miles (800 km).

The Huang River is linked to the Chang River by the Grand Canal (shown above). This famous waterway was begun before 500 B.C. It took workers hundreds of years to complete.

The Ob

The Ob is the second longest Siberian river. Its length is measured from the source of its greatest tributary, the Irtysh River.

In the winter the Ob River freezes over as far south as Novosibirsk, where these boats are.

The big freeze

The Irtysh River begins on the border between China and Mongolia. It runs through Kazakhstan, into Russia, and then flows into the Ob River on its way to the Arctic Ocean. The Ob River is frozen solid each winter. Its **estuary** is blocked with ice from October to June. But in the summer the river is an important route for ships carrying grain and cattle.

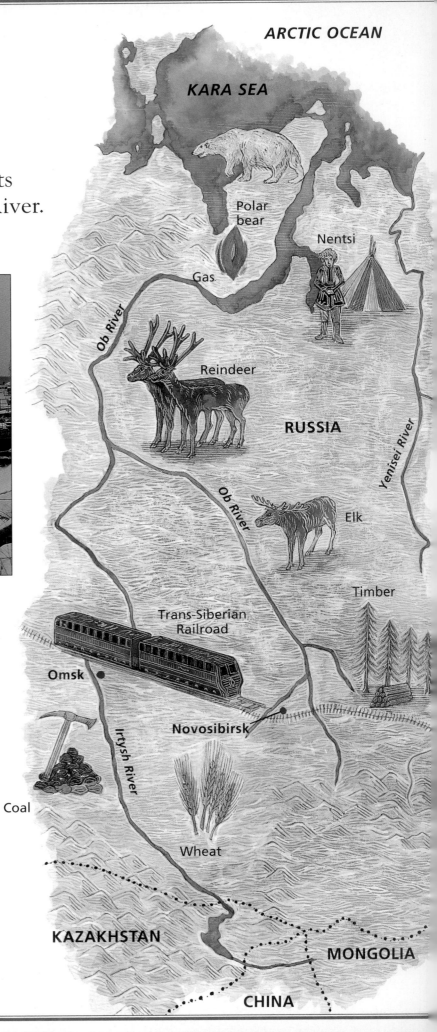

ARCTIC OCEAN

KARA SEA

Polar bear

Gas

Nentsi

Ob River

Reindeer

RUSSIA

Yenisei River

Ob River

Elk

Timber

Trans-Siberian Railroad

Omsk

Novosibirsk

Irtysh River

Coal

Wheat

KAZAKHSTAN

MONGOLIA

CHINA

Railroad cities

The largest city in Siberia lies on the Ob River. It is called Novosibirsk. It grew in 1893 when the Trans-Siberian Railroad was being built. Almost one and a half million people now live in the city. The railroad bridge over the Ob River is the longest on the line. This famous railroad connects Novosibirsk to the biggest city on the Irtysh River, called Omsk.

Life on the Ob

The Khanti and Mansi are two related peoples who live near the Ob River. In the past they went hunting in the winter. In the summer they returned to their villages by the river to fish. Now many of these people work on farms or in factories.

The Nentsi people live farther north. They herd reindeer, hunt, and fish. Many live in wigwams. They used to cover the wigwams in fur and birch bark. Now the wigwams are covered with a **tarpaulin**.

A Nentsi family in front of their wigwam. These people move around the Siberian tundra and forest. Many have now settled in farming villages.

FACTS

LENGTH	3,361 miles (5,409 km)
SOURCE	China–Mongolia border
MOUTH	Russia, into the Kara Sea and the Arctic Ocean

The Paraná

The Paraná River is South America's second longest river after the Amazon. It begins in southeastern Brazil as the Paranaíba and flows south into the Atlantic Ocean.

Country borders

In Brazil, the Paranaíba joins the Grande River to form the Paraná River. Traveling south, the Paraná River forms the border between Brazil and Paraguay. Then it becomes the border between Paraguay and Argentina. After flowing through part of Argentina and past the city of Paraná, the river flows into the Río de la Plata at the border between Argentina and Uruguay.

PARAGUAY

Coffee

Soccer

Toucan

Rain forest

BRAZIL

Cattle

Itaipú Dam

Iguaçu River

Paraná River

Cotton

Iguaçu Falls

Tobacco

Peanuts

Sheep

Paraná

Armadillo

URUGUAY

Tourism

ARGENTINA

Montevideo

Buenos Aires

Río de la Plata

ATLANTIC OCEAN

The spectacular Iguaçu Falls are 2.5 miles (4 km) wide. Just before the Iguaçu River joins the Paraná, water falls 305 feet (93 m) over the Paraná Plateau.

The power of water

In 1991 the world's biggest dam began making electricity on the upper part of the Paraná River. The water drives **generators** that make electricity. The concrete dam is called Itaipú, which means "stone that sings." It took 40,000 people 17 years to build. The dam is on the border between Brazil and Paraguay. Both countries paid for and share the electricity produced by the dam.

Water rushes through the Itaipú dam.

River of silver

Near the end of its journey, the Paraná River flows past the grassy plains called **pampas**. Here **gauchos** herd their cattle. As it reaches the Atlantic Ocean, the river flows into a huge estuary called Río de la Plata, which means "river of silver." Millions of people live on the shores of the estuary. Montevideo, the capital of Uruguay, is on the northern shore, and Buenos Aires, the capital of Argentina, lies to the south. The mouth of the estuary is 140 miles (225 km) wide.

FACTS

LENGTH	3,032 miles (4,880 km)
SOURCE	South-central Brazil
MOUTH	Río de la Plata, Argentina and Uruguay, into the Atlantic Ocean

The Zaire

The Zaire, or Congo, is the second longest river in Africa, after the Nile. Unlike the Nile, the Zaire flows through tropical rain forest and **grassland**. It crosses the equator twice as it heads west toward the Atlantic Ocean.

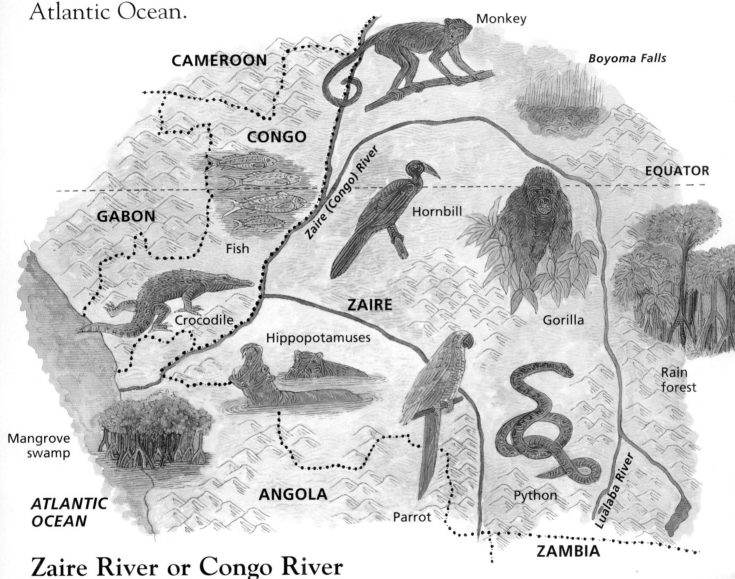

CAMEROON

Monkey

Boyoma Falls

CONGO

Zaire (Congo) River

EQUATOR

GABON

Hornbill

Fish

ZAIRE

Gorilla

Crocodile

Hippopotamuses

Rain forest

Mangrove swamp

ATLANTIC OCEAN

ANGOLA

Parrot

Python

Lualaba River

ZAMBIA

Zaire River or Congo River

The Zaire River begins as the Lualaba River near the border between Zaire and Zambia. It flows north and crosses the equator just before the Boyoma Falls. More water flows over the Boyoma Falls than over any other waterfall in the world. The Zaire River flows on through thick forest toward the country of Congo. For about 373 miles (600 km), the river forms the border between Zaire and Congo. The Zaireans call the river the Zaire, and the Congolese call it the Congo.

FACTS

LENGTH	2,920 miles (4,700 km)
SOURCE	Zaire–Zambia border, southern Africa
MOUTH	Zaire–Angola border, into the Atlantic Ocean

The Zaire River has many rapids and waterfalls, both at the beginning and the end of its journey to the ocean. Ships can travel on the river for just over a third of its length.

Exploring the river

In 1874 an explorer named Henry Morton Stanley began a journey down the Zaire River. It took him nearly three years. At that time, the people of the region were native Africans, mainly Bantu and Pygmies. When the Europeans arrived, they took over the land and ruled the native people. Zaire and Congo became independent countries in 1960.

Fishers use rapids to catch fish in baskets tied on the end of long poles.

Home of the hippopotamus

Herds of hippopotamuses lie under the water in the river. At some places along its banks, the rain forest creeps right up to the water's edge. Gorillas, monkeys, parrots, **hornbills**, **pythons**, and **vipers** all live here.

The Lena

The third longest Siberian river, the Lena, is the tenth longest river in the world. It begins as the Kirenga River near Lake Baikal and flows north to the Laptev Sea.

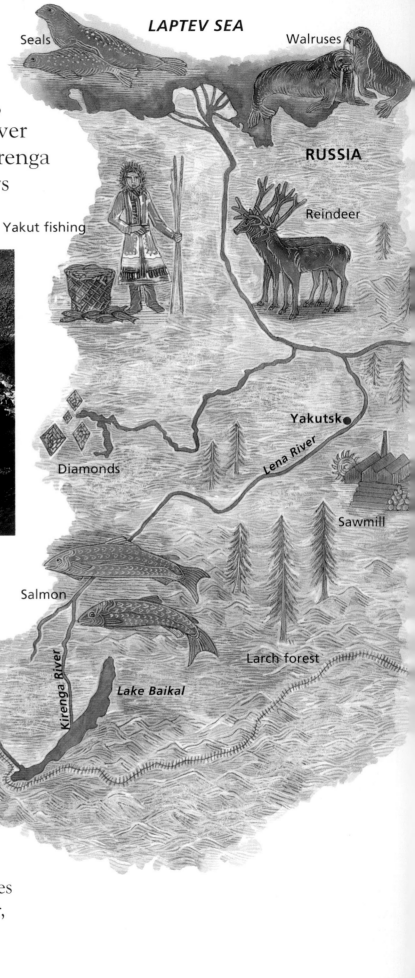

Reindeer travel between summer breeding grounds on the tundra and winter feeding grounds in the forests farther south. Yakut herders move with the reindeer.

Yakut people

The Yakuts live on the Central Siberian Plateau, by the Lena River. The summers are short here, and the winter temperatures are some of the coldest on Earth, at -58°F (-50°C) and even colder. The Yakuts herd reindeer. Some people still live in wooden houses or log huts. But during the long winter, many now prefer to live in apartments in the city of Yakutsk.

LAPTEV SEA

Seals

Walruses

RUSSIA

Reindeer

Yakut fishing

Diamonds

Yakutsk

Lena River

Sawmill

Salmon

Larch forest

Kirenga River

Lake Baikal

FACTS

LENGTH   2,734 miles (4,400 km)
SOURCE   Near Lake Baikal, Russia
MOUTH   Russia, into the Laptev Sea
          and the Arctic Ocean

Sawmill city

There are huge areas of larch forest on the slopes surrounding the Lena. Yakutsk grew up as a sawmill city, using the river to transport timber. For a long time, only wooden houses were built in the city. Now large concrete **pillars** are driven into the frozen soil, so that apartments and other buildings can be built.

The river becomes wider as it flows across the plains of the Yakut region of Russia. There are pillars of rock here that are as tall as trees.

Siberian animals

Like other Siberian rivers, the Lena has plenty of salmon, **sturgeon**, and other fish. The river pours into the Laptev Sea through a wide delta. The delta is home to walruses and seals. Polar bears also roam the frozen arctic ice in search of their favorite prey, ringed seals.

The World's Rivers

Five of the world's ten longest rivers flow through Asia, the biggest continent. Two of the longest rivers are in Africa, another two in South America, and one is in North America. But there are important rivers on the other continents, too.

The Murray-Darling

The Murray is the longest river on the continent of Australia. From the source of its biggest tributary, the Darling, to its mouth in the Indian Ocean, it is 2,330 miles (3,750 km) long. This great river system provides fertile farming land and is used to make hydroelectricity. It winds its way through forests of **eucalyptus** trees (shown right).

The Thames

The Thames River is the second longest river in the United Kingdom after the Severn. Its source is in the Cotswold Hills in the south of England. The Thames flows through London, passing the Houses of Parliament and the Tower of London. It also passes under many bridges, which can cause a problem for large ships coming in from the North Sea. A famous bridge called Tower Bridge solves this problem by opening in the middle and swinging up in the air to let ships through. It was built in 1894. The Thames is 215 miles (346 km) long, so the Nile is almost 20 times longer!

The Colorado

Rivers change the land by carving out patterns for themselves. The Colorado River, in the Southwest, has dug deep gorges and created amazing **meanders**. This one, in Arizona, is called Horseshoe Bend. The Colorado River rises in the Rockies. It flows for 1,450 miles (2,333 km), through Colorado, Utah, and Arizona to the Gulf of California in Mexico. Over millions of years it has carved out the Grand Canyon, the largest gorge in the world. The Grand Canyon is more than a mile (1.6 km) deep, up to 18 miles (29 km) wide, and 280 miles (450 km) long.

The Ganges

Rivers can be holy places. The Ganges River is holy to followers of the Hindu religion. To them, the river is Ganga Mai, or "Mother Ganges." Every year, about a million Hindus go to the Indian city of Varanasi to bathe in the river. They believe its water will wash away their sins.

The Ganges starts 9,843 feet (3,000 m) high in the Himalayas, the world's highest mountain range. Here it is fed by the melting snows. It flows across northern India into Bangladesh, finally emptying into the Bay of Bengal. About 200 million people live in the valley of the Ganges, which is 1,560 miles (2,510 km) long.

Glossary

barge A large boat that has a flat bottom and is used to carry goods

delta The triangle-shaped area at the mouth of some rivers, formed by sand and mud

dyke A bank of earth or other material built to stop a river from flooding

embankment A bank of earth or stone that acts as a dyke

estuary The wide part of a river at its mouth, where the river's freshwater mixes with the ocean's salt water

eucalyptus A tall evergreen tree that grows in warm places

Ancient Egyptians fishing in the Nile

A gaucho riding on the Argentinian pampas

evergreen A tree that has leaves or needles that stay green all year

fertilize To make the soil rich in order to grow good crops

fir A tall evergreen tree with cones and short, flat needles

foothills The lower slopes of a mountain

gaucho A cowboy from Argentina

generator A machine that turns one form of energy, such as the power of water, into electricity

gorge A steep, rocky, narrow pass. A river may run through it.

grassland An area of land covered with grass

hornbill A large bird that has a big bill

hydroelectricity Electric power made by the force of moving water

larch A large tree with cones and needles, which it sheds every year

meander A bend in a river

millet A grass grown for its seeds and used as hay

mouth The end of a river, where it flows into the ocean

pampas The grassy plains of Argentina

pharaoh An ancient Egyptian king

pillar A column

plain Flat countryside without many trees growing on it

plateau A flat area of high land

pollute To damage with poisonous and harmful substances

prey An animal that is hunted by another animal for food

python A large snake that wraps around and crushes its prey

raft A floating platform

rain forest Thick forest found in warm tropical areas of heavy rainfall

Reindeer grazing in the taiga

reserve An area set aside for the protection of animals

river system A large river and all the smaller rivers that flow into it

silt A fine layer of mud and clay

source The place where a river begins

steel foundry A factory where steel is formed into shapes

sturgeon A large fish covered in bony plates

taiga Cold arctic forest of evergreen trees, such as pine and larch

tarpaulin A thick waterproof sheet, often made of cloth and then coated with tar

tributary A small river that flows into a larger one

tundra Flat treeless plains of the arctic, where the earth is always frozen beneath the surface

viper A poisonous snake

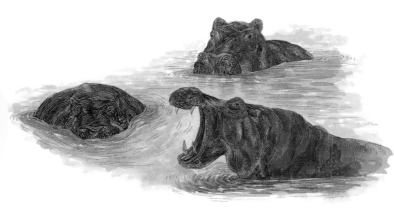

Hippopotamuses wading in a river

Index

Words in **bold** appear in the glossary on page 31.